Paterson
Light and Shadow

Paterson
Light and Shadow

Poems by Maria Mazziotti Gillan

Photographs by Mark Hillringhouse

Serving House Books

Paterson Light and Shadow

ISBN: 978-0-9977797-5-2

Cover photograph: "Great Falls" by Mark Hillringhouse

Serving House Books logo by Barry Lereng Wilmont

Published by Serving House Books
Copenhagen, Denmark and Florham Park, NJ
www.servinghousebooks.com

Member of The Independent Book Publishers Association

Friends of Poets & Writers

First Serving House Books Edition 2017

In memory of
my mother and father, Angelina Schiavo Mazziotti and Arturo Mazziotti,
for all that they taught me about how to love each other and the world.

—Maria Mazziotti Gillan

I want to thank my wife, Linda,
for all her love and encouragement and support over the years,
which has helped me in countless ways.

—Mark Hillringhouse

Contents—Poems

Contents—Photographs

A Note on the Photographs:

The photographs in this book were taken over a twenty-year period starting in the black and white film days with Kodak Tri-X and changing over to digital format by 2006. They have gone from being processed in the wet darkroom as film negatives, to the digital lightroom as raw, tiff and jpeg files.

Introduction to Paterson Light and Shadow

There could be no greater partnership than that between Mark Hillringhouse and Maria Gillan who have lived and taught and wandered in Paterson, New Jersey, where Alexander Hamilton once dreamed of gathering the energy of the Great Falls for the sake of a great industrial base in the new country and where silk mills once flourished making Paterson an important American city and giving employment to generations of immigrants: British, German, Irish, Italian.

Maria is an important American poet in her own right of Italian extraction who gives voice and body to the life of a first generation American woman deeply affected by her southern Italian upbringing. She faced the "American" (Anglo-Saxon) ugly biased treatments of the new immigrants—in schools and elsewhere, with a proud yet angry response. With pride, her mother did piecework (sewing) at home and her father worked in the silk mills until a spinal tumor so weakened him he could no longer work there and did janitorial and watchman work the rest of his life for very little money. Gillan's poems, hauntingly beautiful in themselves in their nostalgic recollections, also document the history of a shy intelligent girl, her family, their struggles and joys, and the entry later by other immigrant groups—Syrian, Dominican, Peruvian, into Paterson and the enormous changes in what became a struggling inner city with echoes of an important and brilliant past.

Hillringhouse's photographs chosen to accompany the poems, are significant works of art in themselves, beautiful, technically brilliant and deeply moving, whether of the falls, the Passaic River, abandoned factories or theaters, houses and streets of old Paterson. He is without doubt, one of the great photographers of America which means that he not only knows how to make a photograph, but is deeply schooled in American history, including its glory and its tragedy—in this case—deeply knowledgeable about the history of its rivers, the falls, the city and its industry and life. This partnership—the alliance of the two of them, Maria and Mark—is seamless and powerful. This is an amazing book.

Gerald Stern
July 28, 2016
7 Gracie Square
New York City

In the City of Dreams: Paterson, NJ

I return to the block in Paterson where we lived when I was
a child, that street with its two- or three-family houses, that street
with the raggedy apartment building on the corner where Irene lived,
Irene with her yellowed teeth, her torn clothes, wrinkled
and soiled, Irene whose family all looked like her, poorer
than the rest of us on the block because her parents drank
and the hallways of the building smelled of urine and where
my mother warned me not to go.

Across the street Judy lived on the second floor over the bar
that her grandfather owned. Her grandmother and grandfather
lived on the third floor. Judy's apartment
had a big terrace, which was really the roof of the bar's
party room, and her parents had money. Between Irene's life
and Judy's, a huge chasm.

Past the old man's candy store, where we did not stop,
our house squatted. We lived on the first floor.
Zia Louisa and Zio Guillermo on the second.
Zio planted a huge garden so I almost believed
we lived in the country. Next to us
there were vacant lots filled with black-eyed Susans
and daisies and wild grasses. Next to the lots
was Big Joey's house where we watched movies
in his backyard on his father's 16mm projector,
all of us sitting on folding chairs or on the grass,
all of us laughing at the cartoon characters prancing
and leaping across the screen. Across the street,
Little Joey lived, little Joey who loved to write,
Little Joey who came to my reading last month
and I did not recognize him. He is almost as old as I am,
though I don't think of myself as old.

Sometimes, I think that little girl who played on 17th Street
is still playing hopscotch or hide-and-seek in the city
of dreams, all of us are still there, frozen in time,
the river stretching ahead of us wide and deep
as an ocean, summer days slow and easy, full
of games and the smell of flowers and Zio's tomato plants.
In the city of dreams no one dies.   We are protected
and safe as though we lived in one of those snow globes,
where when you shook it, the snow fell over us
like small white flowers or stars.

Our Neighborhood in August...

meant chasing fireflies through vacant lots that were knee deep
in daisies and black-eyed Susans and wild grasses.
In the late 40s, 17th Street in Paterson didn't have that city feel
to it with the Riverside Oval on one end and two
and three houses lining the street, the front garden small
with statues of the Blessed Virgin and rose bushes,
or the back and side yards transformed into the immigrants' gardens.

In our neighborhood in August, we played stickball
in the street or hopscotch or jump rope on the sidewalks,
and as dusk slipped its veil over the neighborhood, the kids, Judy,
Little Joey, Big Joey, my brother, sister and I retreated
to our back stoop. Zio Guillermo's garden filled the entire backyard
guarded over by the wind pointers and bird houses he built,
the tassels of corn whispering as they blew in the wind.

Our neighborhood in August was free and open,
the smooth wood of the porch under our legs, the swell
of ripe tomatoes and cucumbers and lettuce, the sky above us,
a huge black bowl crammed with stars, chunky as blocks of ice, how
they glittered and sparkled above us so close we almost believed
we could pluck one from the sky and slip it into a pocket,
like a lucky charm, and carry it with us forever.

The Royle Machine Shop

My father worked at the Royle Machine Shop for years. He was both the janitor and night watchman. Last week, filmmakers took me to the machine shop because I mentioned it in a poem and they shot footage of me reading my poem with the factory in the background. The day after we go there, they send me photos taken that day with Royle Machine Shop on a bronze plaque in the background. The photographer talks the owners into letting him photograph the inside. When I look at the pictures for the first time, I think of my father cleaning that huge space and dragging his crippled leg through his nightly rounds. Was he afraid? He never said. A few days ago, they demolished the factory. The owners did not want to pay the taxes for a building that was empty. The Historical Preservation Commission tried to stay the demolition, but the city refused to waive their taxes, so now, a factory built in 1888 is gone. In its place, only dirt and rubble.

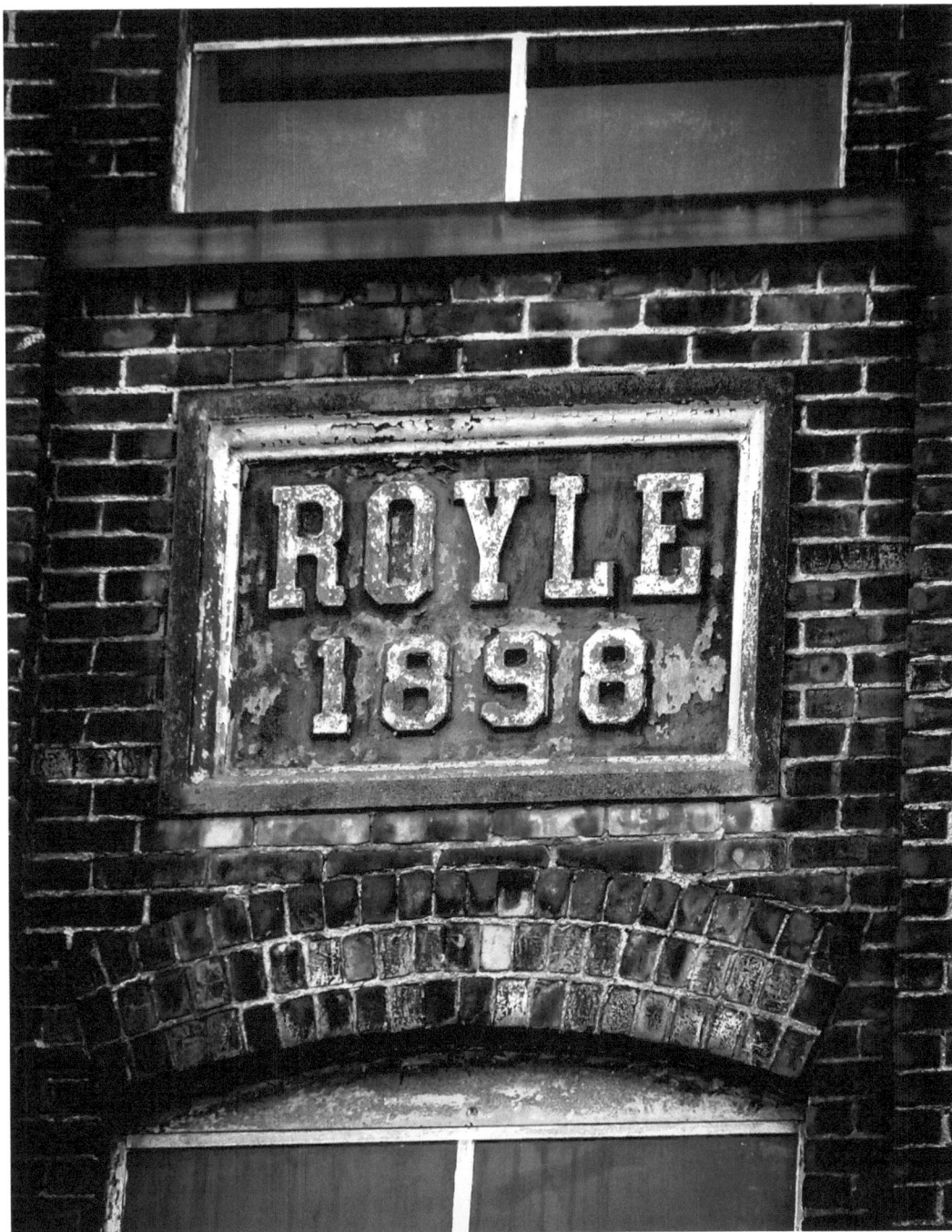

Watching the River Rise

I pull into the parking lot at the Paterson Great
Falls National Historical Park, and listen
to falls roaring like an enraged monster,
though they gleam silver and beautiful,
setting off a cloud of spray, the rain falls
like polished pewter, pounds the blacktop,
the river, muscular and fast, carries with it
broken tree branches that lift out
of the hurling water like arms.
How alive the Passaic River is on this rainy
spring day, even the statue of Alexander Hamilton watches
the falls, though Hamilton appears unmoved, standing
on his pedestal where he has stood for years.
I remember the scene from *The Sopranos*, where they
threw a man over the ledge into the water,
and I look at the falls and the delicate bridge
that spans the water. I have never climbed on it—I am afraid
of heights and the bridge seems too slender to hold
my weight—but I love this spot, love to watch
sunlight shimmer off the falls.
How much of our lives are like that, when
we take a risk to reach out to someone else, to tell
the truth, we are almost dizzy with fear,
balanced on the thin bridge of our own vulnerability,
willing to take a chance, to step on
the span that could lift us to the other side
or let us fall into the rapids below.

Jersey Diners

All the Jersey diners have vanished, those old silver
rectangles with their counter stools that twirled,
their neon lights, their metal tables and fake leather booths.
After we'd go out with a crowd, we'd always end up
at one of those diners, each group wanting to stop
at a different one—West's Diner on Rte. 46 in Little Falls,
Libby's in Paterson, Madison Avenue Diner near
Railroad Avenue. Looking back, I see our young faces
lit by the harsh diner lights,

and only from a distance do we know how protected
we were, how we'd mourn the passage of time,
the loss of so many we loved,
the vanishing of these diners, replaced by malls
and shopping centers, hotels, and big box stores,
the diners glowing only in memory, in all their tacky
glory, and we, our faces still untouched by grief and loss,
caught and framed in the diner's windows.

I Am on the Road Back to Childhood

I am on the road back to childhood, back
to 17th Street and the tenement with the fake
brick siding, back to Zio Guillermo's garden
with corn and tomatoes and zucchini and peppers
and zinnias and marigolds and basil and rosemary,
that fragrant place that made us sure that we lived
in the country. I am on the road back to the 17th Street
kitchen with its big black coal stove and the dangling
one-bulb fixture that lit the table, back to the games
of Monopoly and dominoes and gin rummy that I
played with my sister and brother, back to the aroma
of my mother's homemade bread, back to the meals
she prepared—polenta and spaghetti and meatballs
and sausage and farina—back to the noisy, cheerful
kitchen full of political arguments and laughter, full
of the talk of aunts and uncles, espresso and anisette,
back to small water glasses of wine, back to my father
mixing eggnog for me in a cup, back to my mother sitting
in her rocker, we children leaning over her while she told
us fairy tales from Italy, though her hands were busy
sewing the lining in coats that were dropped off
by the factory each morning and picked up again
the next day, back to a time when we were unaware
of all we didn't have because the arms of our family
were around us and we did not have a TV, that window
into the rest of America, so we were happy with playing tag
in the vacant lot or hide-and-seek in the street, happy
with the evenings on our back stoop where we spoke
in whispers and the neighborhood kids gathered
and summer was an ocean of time we were sure
would never run dry, and the stars, the stars
in the Paterson sky, shone above us, clear and bright
as the future we were sure we could reach out
and hold in our hands.

Public School No.18, Paterson, New Jersey

Miss Wilson's eyes, opaque
as blue glass, fix on me:
"We must speak English.
We're in America now."
I want to say, "I am American,"
but the evidence is stacked against me.

My mother scrubs my scalp raw, wraps
my shining hair in white rags
to make it curl. Miss Wilson
drags me to the window, checks my hair
for lice. My face wants to hide.

At home, my words smooth in my mouth,
I chatter and am proud. In school,
I am silent, grope for the right English
words, fear the Italian word
will sprout from my mouth like a rose,

fear the progression of teachers
in their sprigged dresses,
their Anglo-Saxon faces.

Without words, they tell me
to be ashamed.
I am.
I deny that booted country
even from myself,
want to be still
and untouchable
as these women
who teach me to hate myself.

Years later, in a white
Kansas City house,
the Psychology professor tells me
I remind him of the Mafia leader
on the cover of *Time* magazine.

My anger spits
venomous from my mouth:

I am proud of my mother,
dressed all in black,
proud of my father
with his broken tongue,
proud of the laughter
and noise of our house.

Remember me, Ladies,
the silent one?
I have found my voice
and my rage will blow
your house down.

The Young Men in Black Leather Jackets

Today I am reminded
of the young men
who stood for hours
in front of the candy store
on 19th Street and 2nd Avenue
in Paterson, New Jersey,
the young men in black leather
jackets and tough faces,
their ducktail haircuts identical,
the young men who stared with hard
bright eyes at the girls passing by
and made comments like "Here, chickie, chickie,
c'mere, chickie," their laughter following us
down the street.

One day, as I dreamed my way through
one of the long novels I loved,
their footsteps sounded on the pavement.
The three of them walked in perfect step,
their long legs scissoring as they sang
in their loudest voices:

My Bonnie lies over the ocean.
My Bonnie lies over the sea.
My mother lies over my father's knee
And that's how they got little me.

For years, I remember their song,
the look of terrible mockery in their eyes,
their hatred of women and their need of them,
I remember that it was August. Late. Almost time
for school again. They are seventeen or eighteen;
I am thirteen.

I do not understand their song; I only know
I am ashamed as though I, and not they,
had done wrong.

In the Still Photograph, Paterson, New Jersey, Circa 1950

We are standing in a backyard.
Part of a porch is visible, a lattice
heavy with roses, a small tree.
Beyond the bushes in the background,
a woman with her hand on her hip
stares at us.

My father is young. He squints
into the sun. He wears a white shirt,
a flowered tie, a pair of gabardine pants
and dress shoes. His hair is thick
and crew cut. My mother wears high-heeled
black shoes with a strap across the ankle
and nylons and a black dress
printed with large flowers,
her hair, bobbed and neat.
Her arm, bent at the elbow,
looks strong and firm.
I cannot see her expression clearly,
but I think she is smiling.
Her hand is on my sister Laura's arm,
Laura stands between them.
She is thirteen, her skin clear and beautiful.

My brother, Alex, and I share a small stool
in front of the three grouped
behind us. My long hair drawn back
in a straight line. I sit
behind him. He is about seven,
slim and dressed up in imitation
of my father, except Alex wears

a bow tie. His knees look sharp
and boney through his pants,
his hands clasped together
between his knees.
Even in the standard family picture,
we do not look American.

I think of my mother's preparations:
The rough feel of the washcloth
and Lifebuoy soap against my face,
the stiff, starched feel of my blouse,
the streets of Paterson, old and cracked,
the houses leaning together
like crooked teeth, the yards
that grow larger as we climb the hill,
the immigrant gardens.

We walk back home
in early evening, after the grown-ups
have espresso and anisette
and we, small jelly glasses of juice.
My brother's hand in mine, I pretend
to be grown up. Dreams
cluster around my head
like a halo, while crickets
fill the summer evening
with their shining web of song.

17th Street: Paterson, New Jersey

It was almost a ceremony, the welcoming of company. The aunts and uncles, the espresso pot, the espresso poured in a dark stream into the doll-sized cups set ever so delicately in their little saucers, a small sliver of lemon rind added to float near the top, then the sugar in its bowl, the spoon, midget-sized, made especially to go with those cups and saucers, and the little clink while they stirred their coffee, the men at one end of the table. Sometimes they passed out little glasses, the size of a quarter and almost one inch high, a tiny handle attached, and my father poured whisky or brandy for them, mostly the men, but sometimes the women, too. The children, sitting between the adults, were given coffee in their cups, a drop or two of coffee and lots of milk and sugar, and they listened to the stories about their parents' friends: the wayward children, the wives who were faithful or not, the men who were fools.

Listening, wide-eyed, believing, I learned more in those moments than I could in years of school about laughter and the way of opening up to others and welcoming them in, and of the magic at the heart of ordinary lives, so that ordinary things transfigured them.

Looking back, I see that ever since, I have been searching for that sweetness, the warm bread-baking aroma, the smoothness of oil cloth, its rubbery smell, the open look of my father's face, sparks flying from him in his pleasure, my mother's hand, delicate, the charm of those moments where I rested in the luminous circle of love.

Paterson: Alpha and Omega

I am twelve years old.
I am slim with new breasts
and a bra, size 32, triple A
and black slacks my mother calls dungarees,
but they're nothing like the blue jeans
the popular kids wear;
they're an inexpensive version
of those jeans and in them,
despite my new figure, I feel
awkward and uncomfortable.
I know they are the wrong kind,
and in the world of the seventh grade,
there is only one right kind.

The year I'm twelve I read
every Laura Ingalls Wilder book,
"Little House on the Prairie"
more real to me than the world
of 19th Street:
with its tilted stoop,
the factory across the street,
the girls who wear buckskin jackets
with fringe on them
in which they look like Daniel Boone.

When I think of 19th Street, I think of Ruthie
who used to walk home from PS 18
past my house.
One day, Ruthie walked with me to the top
of the Madison Ave hill.

At 6th Avenue, she turned
to head for the Projects

while I went on to the Riverside Branch
of the library. She was one of the few white kids
in our class who lived in the Projects
and who was not Italian.
She had freckles on her nose,
arrived in PS 18 in seventh grade,
and was lonely.
In one long sentence,
like the kind of sentence that
Faulkner used, one of those sentences
that goes on for paragraphs, she told me
that she was going to leave
Paterson and the Projects
and was going to move in with her wealthy aunt
and have all the clothes she could ever want
and then everyone
would want to be her friend.
Even as she spoke, I knew
she was lying, fabricating
a story she wanted to believe
so desperately
that when she was finished,
she almost believed it herself.
I cringed for her, nodded, agreed.
After that day, she avoided
me as much as she could,
looked past me
as though I didn't exist
and though she must have graduated
with us, I don't remember seeing her again
until we are sophomores at Eastside High School.

I am in Alpha classes.
Most of my classes are on the third floor.
One day, as I am walking into the building,

I see her in the front lobby.
She is standing with a runty-looking boy
in jeans and a black leather jacket.
His pimpled face leans toward Ruthie,
and Ruthie, her back to the wall, reaches up
to him and he kisses her, a long movie-star kiss.
Her skirt is tight and cheap-looking,
her blouse is a see-through nylon,
with her breasts sticking out of it
in obvious little points, but it's her face
I remember best. While he kisses her,
her eyes are open. Accidentally, I look
right into them. I see her cringe,
a flash of shame in her face, and then,
the hot surge of defiance. I know
that she is already lost, probably was lost
even on that day three years before
when we walked up Madison Ave hill
and she told the story of how she would escape
from the tightening ring of her life.

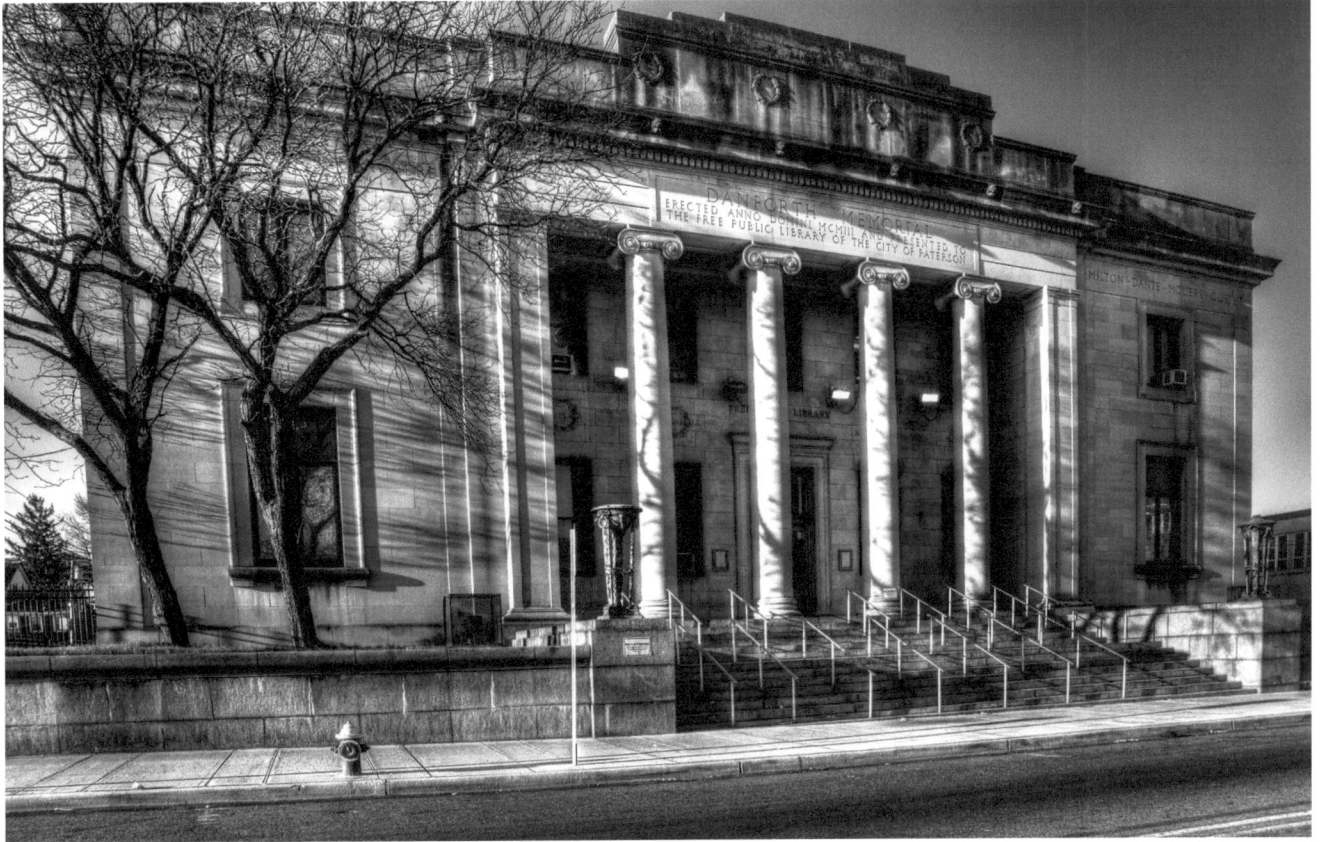

Thinking About the Intricate Pathways of the Brain

This snail shell is smooth and cool
in my hand, smooth as the slide
in the playground at the Riverside Oval,
the silver surface slippery
so that I slid to the ground in a rush
that took my breath away.
The inside shell is reached
through a curved lip
that forms a laughing
or sneering mouth,
and inside, a small protected curve,
and in the deepest
part of it, shadows.

I think if you could travel into it
deep enough, if you could take that journey
to the center, you'd discover
the witches waiting
with their chants and runes,
but if we gave them names,
they'd be able to escape,
like all the fears of which we are ashamed
and all the memories that lie
in the rabbit warrens
of the brain,
pathways that lead
to the witches with their
bags full of the past.

The self that is still
six years old is afraid

of heights
and of the older child
pushing the swing higher
and the laughter and terror caught
in our throats and the sky
washed in blue light moving, moving,
our legs reaching up
toward leafy trees and the perfect
puffy clouds of a July morning.

In Falling Light, Paterson

In falling light, Paterson sky
is an incredible blue so bright
and deep it seems painted on even as it slides
toward pale pink against the ochre brick
mills. I drive past the rococo arches
of the Church painted in lavender and gray,
drive down to Oliver and then, onto Mill,
past Federici's green and decaying
Dublin Spring sculpture
and onto Route 80 where the stars
thicken into clusters in the blazing sky
and the lights of the city float in a sea
of space. The weight
of the day lifts, light as a gauze
shawl, off my shoulders, all
heaviness falling away before the
dizzying panorama, luminous
and vast.

Opening the Door: 19th Street, Paterson

The crumbling cement steps led down to the dark cave
of the cellar where the mouse traps waited
in the corners and the big, iron coal furance squatted
next to the coal bin. My father used a shovel
to scoop the coal out; it made a scraping sound,
iron on cement, and the coal rattling.
When he opened the little door of the furnace
and threw in the coal, the flames
rose up, and the heat poured out.
In the back of the cellar was a room made out
of scrap wood where my father made wine
each summer, the cellar reeking of fermenting wine,
his arms bulging when he carried in the heavy boxes
of purple grapes. I told my brother there was a secret
room in the cellar, like the secret rooms
in the mansions in Nancy Drew novels,
except our house
was an old, imitation Victorian house cut up
into apartments. In my mind, I could open up
the door behind the furnace, and step into a magic
world far removed from the dank ordinary cellar.
The life of 19th Street with its factory workers
and drunks, the people next door who fought
and screamed constantly. The world of my mother's life
where she kept us confined to the front porch,
but through that door, everything
I was not and wanted to be waited for me,
and who knew, who knew to what dangerous,
exciting places it would lead?

Work

Every morning, my father drove me to Manhattan
Shirt Factory on River Street where I worked
in the summer after freshman year. My job
was to take down the number on the inside of the collars
of returned shirts and clip tags to them
and then set them into bins according to the reason
for their return. The shirts were often dirty, sweat stained
and smelly, as though someone had worn them for days
before returning them. The supervisor walked up and down behind
the sorters in the small room lit by bare light bulbs
hanging from cords attached to the exposed beams.
No one spoke and dust was thick in the rancid air.
When the wind was blowing in the right direction,
the smell of the polluted Passaic River filled the room.
The windows, covered by a metal grill, were grimy and caked
with greasy dirt. Very little light entered.
A loud buzzer signaled the start of our half hour lunch.
We rushed outside to sit on the front steps
or stand, leaning against the factory wall,
and eat our lunch. No one talked to me.
The others joked around with one another
and occasionally one would say, "Watch out,
you're embarrassing the college kid," but mostly they ignored me.
At the sound of another buzzer, we retreated
into the darkness of the mill and emerged again
only at four when the workday was over.
In between, we sorted dirty shirts.
I hated to pick them up and I kept trying
to hold my breath so I wouldn't have to smell them.
In a few weeks, the boss came in and told me
he wanted me to work in the other plant packing new skirts
into boxes. The factory was a twin of the first,
except it was on the top of a hill. Finished skirts

came toward me on a conveyer belt
like the kind in dry cleaning stores. I had to lift
each skirt off the rack and pack it neatly
in its special carton. This involved standing up
all day and by four o'clock I was ready to collapse,
my legs and arms aching. Sometimes, a few minutes before
 the ending buzzer was to go off, the harsh voice
of the supervisor would shout "overtime."
The regular workers seemed to me to be gray
and wizened—was it the dust or the noise that did it, overtime,
the other workers were happy for the extra hours,
the time-and-a-half pay, but I thought I'd scream
if I had to stay an extra hour.
My father came to pick me up, and I complained about the place
and how happy I'd be to leave it, and it never occurred to me
that he and my mother had to work in a factory every day
for more than forty-five years. I never heard either one of them
complain, or mention the shouting supervisors, their rudeness,
the lack of light, the incredible noise, the dust, the mindless
repetition of the work or how often they must have felt
like screaming but didn't because they couldn't afford
the luxury. They thought about us and what
they had to do, and kept their heads bent,
their faces hidden, while they worked.

The River at Dusk

Late afternoon. I drive past the Bunker Hill factories
over the new steel girders of the Sixth Avenue bridge.
Through the glossy, silver webwork, I glimpse
the river curving toward downtown Paterson,
the trees over it stark as burnt matches

against the darkening sky.
How beautiful the city is at this hour.
People caught in glass and metal
drive toward lamplight,
the rough brushstrokes of factories in the background.
The river, peaceful and slow, moves as it has
always moved, and at dusk, the rising moon,
like a Lucite dipper, lifts the dark water
into a momentary, exquisite light.

Daddy, We Called You

"Daddy" we called you, "Daddy,"
when we talked to each other in the street,
pulling on our American faces,
shaping our lives in Paterson slang.

Inside our house, we spoke
a Southern Italian dialect
mixed with English
and we called you Papa

but outside again, you became Daddy
and we spoke of you to our friends
as "my father"
imagining we were speaking
of that *Father Knows Best*
TV character
in his dark business suit,
carrying his briefcase into his house,
retreating to his paneled den,
his big living room and dining room,
his frilly-aproned wife
who greeted him at the door
with a kiss. Such space

and silence in that house.
We lived in one big room—
living room, dining room, kitchen, bedroom,
all in one, dominated by the gray oak dining table
around which we sat, talking and laughing,
listening to your stories,
your political arguments with your friends.
Papa, how you glowed in company light,
happy when the other immigrants

came to you for help with their taxes
or legal papers.

It was only outside that glowing circle
that I denied you, denied your long hours
as night watchman in Royle Machine Shop.
One night, riding home from a date
my middle class, American boyfriend
kissed me at the light; I looked up
and met your eyes as you stood at the corner

near Royle Machine. It was nearly midnight.
January. Cold and windy. You were waiting
for the bus, the streetlight illuminating
your face. I pretended I did not see you,
let my boyfriend pull away, leaving you
on the empty corner waiting for the bus
to take you home. You never mentioned it,
never said that you knew
how often I lied about what you did for a living
or that I was ashamed to have my boyfriend see you,
find out about your second shift work, your broken English.

Today, remembering that moment,
still illuminated in my mind
by the streetlamp's gray light,
I think of my own son
and the distance between us,
greater than miles.

Papa,
silk worker,
janitor,
night watchman,
immigrant Italian,

I honor the years you spent in menial work
slipping down the ladder
as your body failed you

while your mind, so quick and sharp,
longed to escape,
honor the times you got out of bed
after sleeping only an hour,
to take me to school or pick me up;
the warm bakery rolls you bought for me
on the way home from the night shift.

The letters
you wrote
to the editors
of local newspapers.

Papa,
silk worker,
janitor,
night watchman,
immigrant Italian,
better than any *Father Knows Best* father,
bland as white rice,
with your wine press in the cellar,
with the newspapers you collected
out of garbage piles to turn into money
you banked for us,
with your mouse traps,
with your cracked and callused hands,
with your yellowed teeth.
Papa,
dragging your dead leg
through the factories of Paterson,
I am outside the house now,
shouting your name.

Perspectives

When I go back to look at it, when the reporter
takes me back and snaps my picture in front
of our house, the house I lived in until I was eleven,
the two family with the extra family hidden
in the dank cellar where the father got pneumonia

and died, the house seems to have grown smaller in size,
the street, too, small and dirty, soda cans and wrappers
in the gutters. The distance too seems shorter from our
house to Pasquale's corner and Burke's Candy Store
where we got ice cream in coated cardboard containers,

vanilla ice cream packed solid and high over the rim
that we ate with a special wooden spoon on the walk home.
In Ventimiglia's vacant lots we played through summers
chasing butterflies we never caught and playing tag
and hide-and-seek. In that field I learned the only nature

I knew, wild daisies and weeds and black-eyed Susans,
the whisper of tall wild grass that hid us,
the freedom of those endless summer days. The field
that was huge and welcoming is covered over now
with asphalt and cement and rows of garages, the earth

plastered over, every inch of it sealed in. The reporter asks
me questions, but my mind is caught in the past, caught
in the scent of Zio Guillermo's garden, the silk tassels
of corn, the dew on the huge tomatoes, the smell of earth
and growing things and Zio Guillermo hiding in the garden

from Zia Concetta's anger. The neighborhood children,
Big Joey, Little Joey, Judy, my sister and brother, gathered
on the back stoop in the summer darkness, telling stories

and smoking punks to keep away the mosquitoes. Often,
in the evenings, my mother would call us inside

and wash us with the stiff washcloths she sewed,
and comb our hair. We'd walk to Aunt Rose's
house to sit under the grape arbor in the evening,
the men playing cards, wine in short glasses before them.

While the men played cards, we sat near the women
who were sipping espresso and talking, listening
to the stories they told till they forgot we were there,
the stories of people we knew or had never met,
stories that come back to me now, tart and sweet,

a taste of mint and sugar, a drop of espresso
in a big cup of milk. Those moments glow
like junk jewelry I buy in thrift stores.
How can I tell this young reporter
what it was like to grow up here?

Her eyes see it as a slum, ratty and poor;
my eyes remember those moments walking home
from Zia Rosa's in the dark, the world soft
and shiny, the stars still visible in the Paterson sky,
the music of stories and words singing in my head.

Holding my brother's hand, I walk ahead of my mother.
I am in love with the evening, the stars, my brother's
hand, the cracked sidewalk, roses climbing fences
and trellises, the vegetables and flowers the immigrants
planted, the stone birdbaths they built, my skin about to burst
in its sweetness, the stories stored up like treasure
that I would find again and again as I grew older.

Cafeteria

In the cafeteria at Eastside High School there was a sour
milk smell that slapped my face when I stepped through

the door. A line of kids circled the room waiting to get
their food. The cafeteria ladies, plump and wearing hair

nets, doled out macaroni and cheese and hamburgers.
I sat at a table with the others who brought their lunch

from home, pulling out my garlicky-smelling escarole
sandwich, or pizza *chiana* or some other Italian delicacy,

and ate shyly in little bites hoping no one would notice
the sharp tang of garlic in the air. Then the voices

and clanking trays and boys clowning with one another
to get the girls' attention rose to a high-pitched roar after

a few minutes, and the cafeteria monitors, teachers
forced to take turns patrolling, blew their whistles.

I usually sat with two or three girls who were
my friends and we would talk and laugh together

quietly. We tried to eat fast and get out. The cafeteria
terrified us. Fights broke out regularly and boys, you

know the kind, loud and teetering on some invisible line
between crazy and just plain brash, would decide

to hound someone, especially someone frightened
or vulnerable. One day three of these boys, they seemed

to be huge to me in retrospect, saw us walking out
of the cafeteria, and one of them in an out of control

manic rage yelled at me, "You're so ugly!
Why don't you get your nose done?" His face screwed up

with disgust, and I cowered away from him, my eyes
filling with tears, his friends laughing, my friends indignantly

walking away from him, telling me not to mind him.
"What a jerk he is!" they said, but I knew that they were

relieved that he had picked on me and not them, all of us,
small and fragile, so unsure, the least breath

could change us forever.

In the Stacks at the Paterson Public Library

When I was fourteen, I asked my father to help me get a job. He called the mayor and asked him for help. My father had worked very hard to get out the vote; so the mayor owed him a favor. When my father said I wanted a job in the Paterson Public Library, the mayor said, "But that pays only 50 cents an hour." My father told me, and I said I still wanted to work in the library. I loved to read, loved the branch library, loved the feel of a book in my hands. I went off to the Public Library where I was told to speak to Ms. Cherry, Supervisor of Circulation. I went there after school, walked from Eastside High to the imposing white columned library, through the marble hall with its curving stair and bronze statues and oil paintings donated by the wealthy old families of the city. Ms. Cherry gave me a sour look, sniffed, and told me quickly what to do; I knew she wasn't happy that I had been palmed off on her and she let me know she didn't like it.

Another young woman started the same day, a tall, beautiful, light-skinned African-American who came from an upper-middle class family. Her father owned a funeral home. She had expensive clothes and straight hair. We both loved books and we liked to talk to each other in the stacks. She knew Ms. Cherry hated us both, but this girl, her name was Anthea, was more articulate and confident than I was. I was incredibly shy and tongue-tied but she'd answer Ms. Cherry back or give her a look that would shut her up immediately. Then Ms. Cherry would scowl at me and find something wrong with what I'd done. She'd yell, and tears would fill my eyes. "Never let her see you cry," Anthea said. "It just makes her happy."

Despite Ms. Cherry, I liked the job, carrying books up into the stacks on the translucent thick glass stairs. Five floors of stacks lined with books. I'd rush up the stairs and shelve the books so I could read for five or ten minutes. Mostly poetry books by Amy Lowell, Edna St. Vincent Millay, Elinor Wylie, e.e. cummings. Light cascading through the stacks, the transparent floors, and onto the poems that soared inside of me, the words seemed to take wing against everything gray and ordinary in my life.

One day Ms. Cherry accused me of stealing a book by Shakespeare. It was missing from where it belonged. Suddenly, all my outrage at the way she treated me, the disdainful way she always spoke to me, rose up, and shy mouse of a girl, I turned on her, my eyes flashing fire. My voice rose so everyone in the library heard, and I said, "I do not steal books and don't ever accuse me of doing something like that again!" my shoulders flung back, my eyes saying if she didn't take it back I'd slug her. She said, "I'm sorry. I'm sorry. Of course you didn't. I don't know what I was thinking," and Anthea, standing behind us, flashed me a huge victory grin.

Learning to Sing

I am in the hallway of the 19th Street house. The front door is a double door. One side is always kept locked, the other side opens when you turn a deadbolt. The door is painted dark brown, a color that is also used for the floor, the banister, and stairs to the upstairs apartment, the door to our apartment. Usually we use the back door into the kitchen, but today I have gone out to get the mail and see a letter for me. I stand in the hallway to open the letter that looks official and is embossed with a return address that says Seton Hall University. The letter is addressed to me.

The letter tells me I have been awarded a full four-year scholarship to Seton Hall University in Paterson, and this scholarship covers four full years of tuition. I shout for my mother, am excited to have won the award. We make so much noise in the hallway that the people upstairs look down to find out what happened.

Suddenly, with my family around me, I realize that I will have to take this scholarship, that I won't be going to the University of Virginia, as I had hoped with its colonnades and old brick and ivy. I had imagined it, though I had not been out of Paterson more than three times in my life, and had no idea what the University of Virginia represented, the kind of people who went there, the way I would have been awkward and out of place. At least, I will not have to go to William Paterson College to major in Kindergarten or first grade teaching as my mother would like. Instead, I can go to Seton Hall, major in English, dream of becoming a writer. When I announce my ambition, my cousin Joey, the accountant, says it's the most impractical thing he's ever heard.

My mother used to say, "Your fate waits behind the door. You cannot see it, but it is there." In that hallway, behind that brown door, my fate came to me: to stay in Paterson, to go to college a few blocks from Eastside High School, to absorb the feel of the city for four more years, to carry the voice of its people, my people, in my head, to hear their stories, and save them to tell. The voices rise in my head, insistent, wanting to be heard, stories that they could never have told, never have found the words to tell them. In my stories, I hear these people who are so much a part of my life, their voices caught like music in my mind. I had to cry a long time before I could learn to sing their songs, as my own.

The Herald News Calls Paterson a "Gritty City"

When I leave Passaic County Community College at dusk,
the sky is the most amazing color—deep violet and luminous,
like an old woman who is smiling suddenly looks young.
The courthouse dome is outlined against the sky,
the rococo arches of the old post office,
the clock tower of the new federal building,
starkly simple, and the clock tower of city hall,
ornate and elegant.

I love the voice of this city, the eyes
of its people, the whooshing sound of the Great Falls,
the old mill that has become a museum,
its brick work shining in sunlight.

I see the old men sleeping in the dumpster,
the prostitute resting against the walls of St. Paul's
Church, the empty crack vials
in the gutter, the transvestites on the corner,
but, under the gritty surface, a fresh energy rises,
and it is the heart of the city—
it beats in the shiny copper of the fountain
in Cianci Street park, in the old men in the Roma Club,
shrewd and wary, squinting against cigarette smoke,
playing Italian card games and drinking espresso.

It beats in the chests of the new immigrants—
Iranians and Columbians, Cubans and Syrians
Dominicans and Indians, carting their hopes to this city
and dreaming, and in the young men with the gangsta pants,
their underwear showing, and in the bravado
of the girl with the braids and the yellow barrettes
and her starched dress and in the little boy

with his torn sneakers and his jean jacket
and the handsome clean lines of his face.
I sing this song for them, for all of them,
the saved and the lost, the ones who will survive
and the ones who will not. I sing for the Jamaican family
and their new restaurant and their hard work
and the young Cuban woman who wants to make money
from her poetry, and for those who will find
the city's heart beating under grit
and who will hear its music
and sing along.

Little House on the Prairie

After I found the *Little House on the Prairie*
books in the Riverside Branch of the Paterson
Public Library, I read them all, my eyes moving
fast across the page, and then read them all
again, fascinated by the family's journey over mountains,
across plains, admiring the courage
it took to travel that huge emptiness to get
to a place they'd never been,

while I sat in Mr. Landgraff's seventh grade
at PS 18 in Paterson; Mr. Landgraff
who was sarcastic, mean, and handsome,
in a white-haired, white-man
kind of way. Mr. Landgraff who preferred
the pretty charming girls. Mr. Landgraff
who thought I was too introverted and shy.
I dreamt my way through seventh grade,
imagining myself in that covered wagon,
though I hadn't left Paterson more than twice,

for in *Little House* I found the bravery
I lacked, reading all evening at home
and walking to school in the morning,
sitting where Mr. Landgraff told me to sit,
crushable as a caterpillar. But after he marked
off my name in his attendance book, I floated
off to Kansas and Nebraska, sure that, like Laura,

I could be brave, that there was a place out there
where I could live a life as extraordinary
and risky as any I read about in books,
far removed from the chalk dust
and quiet despair of seventh grade

with its green black-out shades,
its picture of George Washington,
its scarred and battered desks
that tried to hold me captive.

I Want to Write a Poem to Celebrate

my father's arms, bulging and straining while he carries
the wooden box of dark purple grapes down the crumbling,

uneven cement steps into the cellar of the old house
on 19ᵗʰ Street. The cellar, whitewashed by my mother,

glows darker as my father lumbers past the big coal
furnace and into the windowless wine room

at the back where he will feed the grapes,
ripe and perfect and smelling of earth,

into the wine press. The grape smell changes
as they are crushed and drawn out into fat

wooden barrels, and for weeks the cellar
will be full to the brim with the sweet smell

of grapes fermenting into wine, a smell I recognize
even forty years later each time I uncork a bottle,

an aroma that brings back my father
and his friends' gathering under Zio Gianni's

grape arbor to play briscole through the long July
nights, small glasses before them, peach slices

gleaming like amber in the ruby wine.

City of Memory, Paterson

The city of memory, Paterson, its sky, lavender and purple at dusk, the hills above it, Garret mountain with its dark face and Lambert Castle looking down over the city, its parking lot, the lookout we used to park in when I was in school, the stars over the City, the lights of its buildings, the shadow of NY city in the background while the windows steamed up with our

quick breathing. The city today when I drive down River Street past Our Lady of Lourdes and the Red, White and Blue thrift shop, walk to my building from the lot, past the bail bondsmen signs, and travel agents with signs in Spanish and a flower shop, sporting Spanish words in the windows, past the men in the halfway house next to our building, toothless

men who have the look of old drunks, the seedy-looking young men, their eyes shifting, their hands hanging empty at their sides, this house sad and decrepit where jazz music streams out of the open window each morning. At noon I walk back out of my building, down Ellison to Main where the stores of my youth are gone, replaced by signs that shout

"Dollar Store" and "Bargain" or "Final Going Out of Business Sale," and where in front of each store sits one man on a high ladder to watch the people going in and out of the store to make sure they aren't stealing anything and the clerks who are rude to their customers because they are poor, and I remember Paterson when I was young, Meyer Brothers

Department Store with its lovely displays, Chanel #5 perfumes, Naturalizer shoes, creamy leather handbags, its elevator operators who wore white gloves and announced the merchandise on each floor and Quackenbush's Department Store, not as fancy as Meyer Brothers but almost, where sometimes we'd stop in the restaurant at the bottom of the curved stair and have an ice cream sundae, though that was later when I was already grown up, and not when I was still a child and my mother would take the three of us, my brother, sister and me downtown while she bought freshly ground coffee in the coffee store and went to pay on time for a refrigerator at Quackenbush's. When I'd speak to my mother in Italian she'd say sh-sh and people would pass and say why don't they speak English? They should go back to where they came from as they do now when people speaking Spanish or Arabic pass by. Once when I was a teenager I went to Quackenbush's with my mother when she was trying to buy

support hose and the clerk was rude and insulting to her, and I stepped in, my voice raised, my arms on my hips, said "Don't ever speak to my mother or any other customer like that again. I want to speak to the manager." My mother pulled on my arm saying sh-sh, but I wouldn't stop, fury like molten lava taking over my body, my mind, at all the injustice

in the world, at the way being poor and foreign is a crime and the way the poor take it, think they don't deserve anything better, saying sh-sh to their children whose rage finally refuses to be silenced.

I Open a Box

...and find inside a picture,
of myself as a child, sitting
on a small chair, wearing overalls
and shoes that must have been
hand-me-downs because they are
so worn the sole is coming loose.
I am no more than 18 months
old and cannot have been walking
all that long. I am squinting
into the sun, my nose crinkling
with effort the way it crinkles now
when I am trying to see in bright light.
Behind me, the six-family tenement
where I was born on 5th Avenue
in Paterson, the rickety stairs rise up
three floors, the porches tilt a bit
as though they might fall off
if someone were to jump on them
too hard. My mother delivered
me herself in this coldwater flat.
The doctor didn't get to her in time,
and when he did, he, in his pressed
and starched white shirt and expensive
suit and polished shoes, stood at the door
and didn't enter the room. My mother
cut the cord and washed me off, wrapped
me in a clean blanket. When she
was dying years later, she said,
"The doctor didn't even come into
the room. He washed his hands, wiped
them on one of the rough linen towels
I brought from Italy, stood in the doorway.
"You'll be okay," he said, and left.

"Oh, well," my mother said, "I think
he was afraid of catching it."
"Catching what?" I asked.
"Poverty," she said.

What Did I Want

What did I want as I sat in that dusty 6th grade classroom
at PS 18? Outside the windows rain, gray and bleak.
Black smoke from the factory across the street
stained the sky. Inside the room, Mrs. Richmond paced
in her high heels and tight sweaters and too bright lipstick.
She was quick to criticize, quick to turn her eyes into blue ice
that flashed and sparked. I never wanted her to look at me,
but there was no escape. The day stretched out taut, ready
to snap, and often I'd drift away from her monotone

to dream of following covered wagons across plains
to places I had never been and had little hope of going,
but in my mind, I could imagine what those places
would be like, could almost see the buffalo,
as if they were roaming the streets of Paterson.

I did not know how hard it was to leave behind
the lives we were born to, the Italian neighborhood,
the cracked and broken sidewalks, the brick factories
where our parents worked, how this gray life marked us
as clearly as a scar on our faces. It was there in the way
we walked, the sound of words in our mouths.

Only in books was there a path to take us away
to a place where all things were possible,
where nothing mattered except the bright bird
in our minds who could lift up and soar away.

Going to the Rivoli in Downtown Paterson

When we were growing up, we went to downtown Paterson
to the Rivoli Theater on Main Street to see the latest movies
and the stars we loved—Rock Hudson, Doris Day,
Tab Hunter—the theater ornately carved with cherubs
and angels, elaborate moldings and glass chandeliers
and velvet curtains. That was when Paterson still thrived,
before the first shopping center opened in Elmwood Park
and then on Rte. 4, the Garden State Plaza and the Bergen
Mall, and people stopped taking the buses into downtown
to shop at Meyer Brothers where the elevator operators
wore white gloves and announced the goods on each floor,
before they stopped going to Quackenbush's with its curving
stair that led to the restaurant where people with money
(or more money than we had) would stop for lunch
or to Berman's for cashmere sweaters or to the Rivoli
or the Fabian to watch movies. That was in the fifties before
the wealthy people from the Eastside section moved out
to Fair Lawn or Glen Rock, before they moved to places
where they had to have a car because there was no
public transportation, before poor people started moving
into Paterson, people poorer than we were, the immigrants
who crowded into the ethnic neighborhoods
like the Totowa section or Riverside in the thirties and forties, and who
by the late fifties moved out, too, to blue collar suburbs, looking
for more space, bigger gardens, before they, too,
all bought cars and stopped walking or taking buses
and trains. On Saturdays, after school when I was a girl,
we'd take the bus downtown and we'd walk up and down
Main Street in and out of stores. We never bought anything,
but we liked wandering the aisles of Meyer Brothers,
spritzing ourselves with perfume, if we dared, and smelling
the leather purses we couldn't afford. Then we'd retreat
to the Rivoli, to the elegance of the theater, to that moment

when they'd dim the lights and the movie would flash onto
the huge screen and we'd leave behind our ordinary lives
and enter the world of the film, a place where people lived
lives that were magical and glittering, a place
where people could have whatever they desired
and never have to count the costs.

December Dusk

A precariousness steals over things
at dusk when darkness bleeds the light away
and our shadows stretch their long fingers.
Objects change then. Even the sound
of the old house changes and grows dim.

The trees' menace creeps along the floor
while fear brushes against the bones.
We draw the curtains, light the lamps;
they cannot contain it, this whisper
which curls around us. We shiver at our image
in the darkening glass, our eyelids
flutter, our blood beats
against our thin skins.

I Grew Up With Tom Mix

I grew up with Tom Mix and Roy Rogers, Hopalong Cassidy,
the Lone Ranger and Tonto. The good guys always wore white hats so
it was easy to tell them from the bad guys. Little boys had cap guns
and six shooters with holsters. Some of the boys

even wore cowboy vests and boots. We listened to the brown
counter top radio, made of imitation mahogany, tan netting
over its speakers. We'd pull kitchen chairs up to the counter
on the built-in china closet, and in the kitchen,

heated by a huge black iron coal stove, we'd listen to the programs.
We had to imagine their horses, their white hats, miles of open
space and mountain ranges we had never seen, our imaginations
filling in the gaps left by whatever we didn't know, the places

we'd never been. The radio let us leave behind that Paterson
apartment, transported us to the great valleys of the West,
to covered wagons, the saloons, the shootouts on dirty, unpaved
streets. Our real world had boundaries built by my Italian parents

and the streets we were allowed to travel, the Riverside Oval
on one end and 4th Avenue and Mastalia's grocery store
and Burkes's candy store on the other, and in between, the children
we played with each day. But huddled near the radio we could go

anywhere, be anyone, imagine lives so different from our own,
exciting and dangerous, where at the end of each program
we knew no hero we loved and admired ever died.

Graduating from PS No. 18

In the photograph of our class in PS No. 18 in Paterson, NJ,
we are wearing our graduation dresses, the ones we sewed
ourselves, white eyelet with little cap sleeves and a nipped
in waist. We had to make our dresses in sewing class
and we took four or five months to finish them. Mrs. Z
taught us each step. By the time I finished it and brought it
home to be ironed, it was rumpled and filthy, the white dingy
and soiled. My mother had to take the dress apart and sew it
again but not before she washed it carefully by hand. "I had
to wash it three times," she said, "to get it clean."

In the photograph the dress looks fine. I am wearing a corsage,
one yellow rose, all the girls wearing the same flower. I am thirteen.
I called myself slim, but the others called me skinny or skinny bahlink.
I drank milkshakes to try to gain weight, but no matter how much I ate,
I weighed 94 pounds even with my shoes on.

In the photograph we all looked so fresh and hopeful, though what
did I know? How many were lonely or uncertain, how many afraid?
In our white graduation dresses we were what we were supposed
to be, looked the way we were supposed to look, while inside us all,
hope and terror, trembled like small white birds.

All His Life My Father Worked in Factories

or mills as we called them, back when Paterson
was the silk capital of the USA and was known as Silk City.
When my father was thirty, he had a large tumor on his spine,
and after the doctors at St. Joseph's removed it
he spent three months in the hospital and then a year
at home. He couldn't work and wouldn't let my mother apply

for welfare so we lived for a year on $300, and while $300
in 1943 was a lot more than it is now, it still wasn't enough
for a family of five to live on. We ate spaghetti and farina
and my mother's homemade bread every day. When my mother
was dying, she worried that the year without money–
when she couldn't give my sister five cents to buy milk in school–
was why my sister got rheumatoid arthritis at thirty, a disease
that progressed, eventually invading her lungs and eyes.

 After the surgery my father had a limp that became gradually
worse as he grew older. He was no longer strong enough
to lift heavy rolls of silk, so he got a job as a janitor
in Central High School and when that became too much
for him, he took a job watching the pressure
gauges on steam boilers to make sure they didn't explode.
All his life, my father walked, dragging that dead leg behind him.

All his life, he worked menial jobs, though he did income taxes
each year for half the Italians in Riverside by reading
the two-hundred page income tax book, and he could add,
multiply and divide in his head faster than an adding machine.
He was fascinated by politics and read news magazines
and newspapers, and knew the details of world crises and war.

When I was a girl, I worked in factories during the summers

and I moaned and complained about how boring it was,
how dusty and tiring, how I'd shoot myself if I had to do this job
for one more day, and I think of my father with his sharp intelligence,
forced each day for fifty years to work eight hours a day at jobs
so repetitive they would have bored a mouse, and the way
he never complained, never said I can't do this anymore,
instead he just kept working, knowing he had to do it
so his children would have the soft lives he never had.

The Ducks Walk Across River Street
Paterson, New Jersey

Yesterday, a family of ducks crosses River Street.
All the cars, in both directions, stop to let them go by,

their black heads proud in the air, their beaks pointed
ahead, straight and self-satisfied. They do not hurry.

They walk as though they owned the world, two grown
ducks, three ducklings, two more ducks taking up the rear.

You'd think they lived on some curvy lane
in the English countryside, somewhere near Wordsworth

Cottage, perhaps, instead of on the Passaic River, reeking
of garbage, redolent of waste, near the edge of River Street

with its thrift shop and boxing gym and car wash
and its gaggle of homeless men who sit in broken down

chairs on the edge of the river, as though they, too,
were at some expensive resort. How self-contained

the ducks are, all of us watching them, the people
in their cars heading to work, the homeless men

mumbling or staring at the trees trailing their long fingers
in the river, the ducks certain in their smooth feathers

that the road and the river are theirs by right
as they move graceful as dancers onto the water

and let it lift them into the dazzling morning light.

The Passaic River

Driving over the Lincoln Avenue Bridge into Paterson
this icy December morning, I see two men leaning over the bridge railing
with their fishing poles. They have carried their fishing equipment
in a milk crate. I am surprised to see them there, fishing in the polluted
water. I wonder what they plan to do with those fish, am tempted
to go back and ask them, but drive on down River Street, past the thrift
shops and used tire lots, past Third Avenue where the shoemaker's shop
used to be when I was a child. If I made a left and turned the corner
onto 17th Street, I'd be on the street where I grew up. My father
used to tell me about the Passaic River where he swam in 1922, when he
came to the US from Italy, he and his friends picnicking on the shore, all
of them young, unmarried, exuberant. My father worked in the silk mills,
but they did not make the connection between the dye houses spilling waste
into the river and jumping off the river's edge. "The river was so beautiful. You
could see the fish swimming in it, and the banks were lined with willows," he said.
"Sometimes, we'd walk up to the Falls. After it rained, they'd be so powerful.
We had a good time, though we didn't have money. Once in 1926, we
went on strike and marched up Fifth Avenue to ask for five cents more an hour.
The owners sent the police out and they came with their night sticks, hitting us
until the crowd broke up. One hit me on the head, and I was bleeding
as I ran away. We didn't get our five cents more an hour,
but I'm glad we tried."

Maria Mazziotti Gillan is a recipient of the 2014 George Garrett Award for Outstanding Community Service in Literature from the Association of Writers & Writing Programs (AWP), the 2011 Barnes & Noble Writers for Writers Award from Poets & Writers, and the 2008 American Book Award for her book, *All That Lies Between Us* (Guernica Editions). She is the founder/executive director of the Poetry Center at Passaic County Community College in Paterson, NJ, and editor of the *Paterson Literary Review*. She is also director of the Binghamton Center for Writers and the creative writing program, and professor of English at Binghamton University-SUNY. She has published 22 books, including *What Blooms in Winter* (NYQ Books, 2016); *The Girls in the Chartreuse Jackets* (Cat in the Sun Books, 2014); *Ancestors' Song* (Bordighera Press, 2013); *The Silence in an Empty House* (NYQ Books, 2013); *Writing Poetry to Save Your Life: How to Find the Courage to Tell Your Stories* (MiroLand, Guernica Editions, 2013); *The Place I Call Home* (NYQ Books, 2012); and *What We Pass On: Collected Poems 1980-2009* (Guernica Editions, 2010). With her daughter Jennifer, she is co-editor of four anthologies. Visit her website at *www.mariagillan.com.*

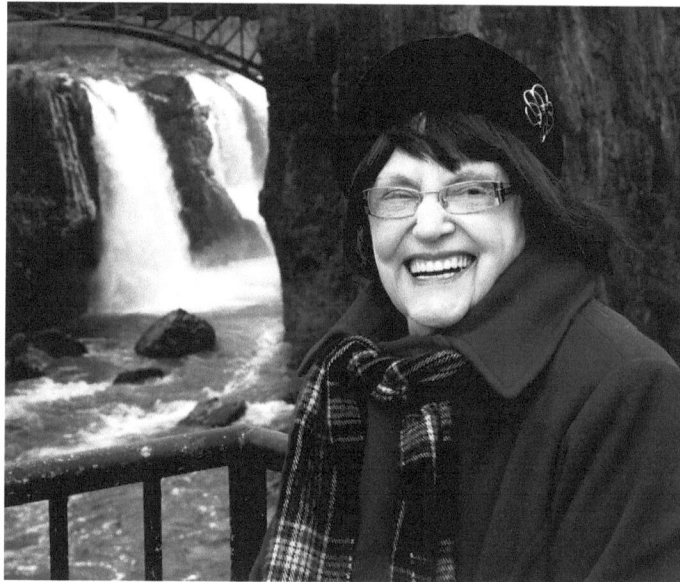

Mark Hillringhouse: is a published poet, essayist, and photographer whose works have been widely exhibited in area galleries. His photography and writing have been published in *The American Poetry Review, The Literary Review, The New York Times, The New Jersey Monthly, The Paris Review*, and in many other journals, books, anthologies and magazines. He was the founding editor of *The American Book Review*, and a contributing editor for *The New York Arts Journal*. Thrice nominated for a Pushcart Prize, and a three-time recipient of a New Jersey State Council on the Arts Fellowship, he has won several awards for poetry and photography including the National Parks Calendar photography contest and the Soho Arthouse Gallery's "Captured! A Moment in Time" exhibition. His film documentary with collaborator Kevin Carey on the life of local Salem poet Malcolm Miller, titled *Unburying Malcolm Miller*, was released in 2017 and screened at the Massachusetts Poetry Festival. His book of poems and photographs titled *Between Frames* was published by Serving House Books. He is a member of the English and Fine Arts Department at Passaic County Community College. Visit his photography Website: http://mhillringhouse.zenfolio.com

Photograph by Chris Lovi

Maria Mazziotti Gillan Acknowledgments

The Girls in the Chartreuse Jackets (Cat in the Sun Books, 2014)
In the City of Dreams: Paterson, NJ
Our Neighborhood in August...
The Royale Machine Shop
Watching the River Rise
Jersey Diners
I Am on the Road Back to Childhood

What We Pass On: Collected Poems 1980-2009 (Guernica Editions, 2010)
Public School No. 18, Paterson, New Jersey
The Young Men in Black Leather Jackets
In the Still Photograph, Paterson, New Jersey, Circa 1950
17th Street: Paterson, New Jersey
Paterson: Alpha and Omega
Thinking About the Intricate Pathways of the Brain
In Falling Light, Paterson
Opening the Door: 19th Street, Paterson
Work
The River at Dusk
Daddy, We Called You
Perspectives
Cafeteria
In the Stacks at the Paterson Public Library
Learning to Sing
The Herald News Calls Paterson a "Gritty City"
I Want to Write a Poem to Celebrate
City of Memory, Paterson

Ancestors' Song (Bordighera, 2013)
Little House on the Prairie
I Open a Box

Going to the Rivoli in Downtown Paterson

Paddlefish 2013 #7
What Did I Want

The Place I Call Home (NYQ Books, 2012)
I grew Up with Tom Mix
Graduating from PS No. 18
All His Life My Father Worked in Factories
The Ducks Walk Across River Street, Paterson, New Jersey

The Great Falls: An Anthology of Poems About Paterson, New Jersey
(edited by Maria Mazziotti Gillan, Executive Director, The Poetry Center at Passaic County
Community College, 2014)
The Passaic River

Winter Light (Chantry Press, 1985)
December Dusk

Mark Hillringhouse Acknowledgments

Some of these photographs have appeared in gallery exhibits in New York and New Jersey, and have been featured in many magazines, journals and newspapers across the country, as well as in several books, including—

Between Frames Poems & Photographs by Mark Hillringhouse published by Serving House Books.

The "Great Falls Infrared" photograph won the U.S National Park's Calendar contest for 2012 and is the official Great Falls National Park brochure photograph. A poster reproduction of this photograph is available at the Great Falls Visitors' Center, or from my website mhillinghouse.zenfolio.com.

I want to thank George Tice, my mentor in photography, for his inspiration to keep shooting in the hallowed precincts of Paterson. His black and white large format fine art photographs of urban landscapes taught me a great deal about the haunting beauty of what remains.

www.ingramcontent.com/pod-product-compliance
Lightning Source LLC
Chambersburg PA
CBHW042011090426

42811CB00015B/1616